Beside Still Waters

໒ຉ

I0158586

Joseph Raffa

Beside Still Waters
Author: Joseph Raffa
Editor: Teena Raffa-Mulligan

ISBN 978-0-9872276-7-6

Printed by CreateSpace, an Amazon.com company
Available from CreateSpace.com, Amazon.com and other
retail outlets

Text © copyright Joseph Raffa
This publication is © copyright. No part of this book may be
reproduced by any means without written permission from
the publisher.

CONTENTS

✌⊱

FOREWORD

ESIDE STILL WATERS. The imagination
stirs. A vision appears of a small lake,
surrounded by reeds, bushes and trees.
Mirror-like, the surface of the lake, softly
reflecting the sunlight and the green surrounds.
Not a whisper of a wind stirs to ripple the surface.
The reeds are motionless, gracefully bending to
touch the water or stand upright in the sunlit air.
Water birds drift, unhurried, slow motion their
movements, leaving the barest wake of ripples. So
graceful and serene.

An observer sits by the side of the lake,
entranced by the peaceful scene. The sun shines
warmly on bare skin, the pleasant sounds of
insects caress the hearing. Everywhere, the
blissful presence of life in a quiet mood.

Such are the still waters that many long for. The still waters of the spirit are the deepest stillness of all. Those who go there lose touch with the senses, with their surrounds, with the self they know. Yes, even with thinking and feeling. Reason, descriptive words, are speechless in the presence of this stillness.

Here, birds do not fly, nor call to one another — nor grasses grow, or trees reach for the sky. Indeed, where is the sky, the wind, the sunshine, the clouds that move? Nowhere in sight. And human observers? They too vanish in this stillness, leaving not a trace.

These are the still waters that bring new life to mankind, that lay claim to the heart and redirect the mind. These are the waters of peace, of love, of true togetherness that lift mankind to exalted, divine heights of being and living.

Because of the still waters of the spirit, inspiration flows and the following words were written. May they inspire you to reach out for the still waters of the spirit.

Joseph Raffa, 11th April, 1995

WHAT TOOK ME THIS WAY?

AS A CHILD, I considered the place where I was born a vast, interesting playground. Particularly the ocean, the beaches and sand dunes. The surrounding bushland too was a place of fascination. And so, from the time I was old enough to wander on youthful legs, I played at will.

Not for me then any intention to express more than play. I wasn't drawn by longings to do great things, to be a doctor or scientist or to give out meaningful messages through the written or spoken word.

Schooldays were tolerated because they were a must, not because I considered them a preparation for the time that lay ahead. They were just a distraction that took me away from the places I loved.

Teenage years continued in the same vein. Work was necessary to pay my way, not as a stepping stone to greater achievements in the hierarchy of the workplace. My main focus after work was play — dancing, with the opportunity to flirt with the delightful teenage lasses there, playing basketball, competitive swimming, socialising with and enjoying the companionship of lads much my own age.

This merry-go-round of fun and games only lasted till the advent of World War 2. Its brutality, destruction and cruelty disrupted the tranquillity of day to day living even here in Western Australia, though we were far from the main areas of combat. Before this, I hadn't bothered much about the influences that circulated the planet, affecting humans in diverse ways. And with marriage after the war, play as number one priority in my life began to fade and take a secondary role. Not that I didn't try to hold onto my childish aspirations of having fun, but change was proceeding all around me. Friends were drifting away and settling down to a new life. Sport was being left behind and more serious considerations were coming to the fore.

Life had decided I was to grow up and mature in a different way than just through the passage of years and the accumulation of experience. The adult world is far removed from that of a child's. There is less protection in making decisions, in taking responsibility and facing what follows.

The carefree life I formerly knew faded rapidly. Discontent reared its stubborn head. The world was in ferment. Immigrants, eager to escape from the mess and destruction that was Europe immediately after the war, were pouring into the port of Fremantle where I lived. New technology was surging into the marketplace, construction burgeoned here and there as the nation switched from a wartime focus back to a peacetime one. There was excitement in the air that humanity was going places — somewhere special.

But sadly, tensions and confrontations continued after the end of the war. Former enemies became friends, comrades in arms became enemies and the threat of nuclear annihilation hung constantly over our heads. Wars, strife, hijacks, assassinations of national leaders, morality going haywire, going any which way that humans wanted to take it — all the things the human heart didn't want, that's what we lived with.

The darkness of the post-war years hardly lifted. Some sort of faith, not necessarily religious, a belief in the accustomed continuity of life, that it would somehow go on and we with it, carried us through. Meanwhile, the planet trembled.

The resilience of human nature is amazing. The courage of ordinary people to endure, likewise so. Life did go on and in this little corner of the world the worst of what was happening elsewhere passed us by. Still, within me discontent grew, not only with what was happening elsewhere, but also with my life. Change was proceeding with bewildering rapidity, affecting every social aspect of human living. Not only the outer but also the inner, the expectations, the ideas, the moral basis that we had taken so much for granted.

Humans were being tossed along by events they could hardly control. They were reacting on the international level rather than controlling the course of events. The way ahead was uncertain. Where were we going? What did humans want and expect from their lives?

It was to find some kind of personal answer, something that had practical value in daily living, that drew me away from the usual pursuits. I embarked on a new adventure in living. This was to be an inner journey, not an outer one. I set my sights on the discovery of the Silent Heart of mankind, something I was introduced to by the written word. This offered much in the way of a deeper meaning, insights and understanding that would arise if the journey was fruitful and yielded its harvest of realisation.

I had nothing to lose, except the self I had so carefully nurtured till then. Discontent with my lot was a powerful incentive. I hadn't a clue as to what kind of preparation was needed but with the enthusiasm of youth I set sail to the promised land of self-discovery.

And slowly, painfully at times, the ground was prepared for what would eventually be a yielding of the self and the opportunity for something higher to reveal its nature.

∾ঌৎ∽

A SEAGULL RETURNS TO THE SILENCE

THE STRUGGLES OF the dying gull were sad to see. Borne helplessly towards the shore by a gentle breeze and the flowing motion of the water, it drifted, wings outstretched, head hanging limply backwards, beak open. Now and again it made a desperate attempt to flutter its limp wings but the effort was beyond it.

It floated almost lifeless, rising and falling with the gentle swells, eyes closed; waiting, waiting for the peace of death to claim it and take it back to where it belonged — back to the great unknown.

I sensed a resignation about the gull, a subdued acceptance of the inevitable as if the force drawing it away from the world it knew was too powerful to be resisted. With the patience engendered by the Eternal it awaited the end while its brother and sister gulls wheeled above or floated nearby, slightly agitated, knowing in the way that birds do that death was at hand.

The Universal, knowing no death but only eternal life, enfolded the feeble gull into its all-embracing silence, absorbing it deep into the being from whence it first arose with wings of joy, eager to be active. It lived fully as a bird does, sharing with its kind the feel of sun and wind, the sight of wave following wave, floating on the crests or flying high, wheeling and turning, diving arrow-like into the water, rising with a fish in its beak.

Surely life has consequence even for a bird if it has tasted all this even for only a short time. Is there need for deep sadness at its going? Nature prepared all for it, fashioned its wings, its body; supplied the seafood it hunted, air to fly in, the sea to rest on and the seashore to forage along. That which has given so much surely cannot be condemned for taking it all back if that is the way things are.

So, my children, put away your sadness. The gull has gone but others remain to delight us with their ways. All things are lonely in death if one gazes only on the outer face of nature's handiwork, but to those who are blessed with awareness of her inner being there is the conviction of a deep togetherness even in death.

(*Written after our young children were distressed at the sight of a gull dying slowly on an almost placid river. It was too far out to retrieve so we had to let it be.*)

❧

AN OCEAN INTERLUDE

IT'S SO EXHILARATING to stand on the seashore when strong winds blow. The ocean surface is storm tossed and grey, white-topped waves rise and fall, the wind surges, fresh and free moving.

Overhead, patches of blue sky show between the cloud masses. Along the horizon, where sea and sky seem to meet, the sense of space expands and drifts dreamlike, stirring strange emotions deep within.

A longing arises to leave present time and city confines — the denseness of a fleshly body, the surging flow of thoughts that are a part of the self to which I am attached.

Another vista opens out — of lighter living, of glowing awareness, of wandering rocky shorelines, of fresh ocean breezes, of islands breaking out above the surface of the sea, clouds overhead, flowing, shadows cast across the ocean.

No sense of an enclosed self, of past memories, intrudes to mar the serenity of what unfolds. Just resplendent Being, alive with a lightness.

Other beings interweave within my vision, faces alight with love. A joyous greeting passes between. Being intermingles with Being, the joy of spiritual contact, of happiness unrestricted.

A Lightness observes. The delight of an awareness not clouded over with overriding thoughts, taking in the overall scene, extending into it.

The fresh wind blows through me. The sky, clouds and sea join with me in a spiritual symphony played by the Oneness of Life. Such a longing stirs in me, too exquisite for words.

But the present time is overpowering. It draws me back into the flesh, into the self, such as I know it. This is my present incarnation. There is no escape from it, except fleetingly when spirit takes wings and leaves the self, to roam elsewhere, where flesh and thought cannot go.

Such a delight, the moments when ocean vistas take me into a dreamlike world that sparkles with its own light and reflects an enchanting presence, not only of colours and forms but a sense of something deeper.

Author's note: Strange feelings stirred me to write while down at the seashore walking the dogs. By the time I returned home, the freshness of the occasion had passed. Still I recorded what I could but words cannot bring to life the depth, the freshness, the colour and presence of what unfolded for me.

೪ು೪

IT BEGAN AT THE SEASHORE

THE SEA BREEZE came in with a rush. It scattered the hot air, replacing it with fresh breezes that brought the smell of the sea over the land. The temperature rapidly dropped. Listless people, feeling the freshness, breathed sighs of relief and became active again. Along the coast the breeze poured in from the sea, gusty and laden with coolness. It grew in intensity and people drifted away from the beaches where earlier they had sought refuge from the blistering heat in the cool ocean water. Stinging particles of beach sand were on the move now, striking bare skin with the insistence of angry insects biting. The cool wind became quite cold. Increasingly powerful gusts lashed the water, sending it racing shoreward, scattering it there into spray and surf.

The retreat from the beach became a rout. People hurried away, driven off by blustery wind and stinging sand. Finally, bleakness took over the deserted beaches. Streamers of sand twisted and whirled snakelike over the dunes. Stray pieces of paper raced helter skelter. Water frothed, hissed, surged and splashed. The wind churned the sea and grey clouds came scudding over from the west, blanketing the sun, covering its former fiery face with greyness. Shadows cast by the clouds raced over the sombre sea. They met the land, raced across and were lost in the distance of the faraway hills. Broken clouds merged into banks and the banks into one vast, unbroken mass. As far as the eye could see the sky was covered, its former blueness gone and all around was the agitation of sea and wind, sand and quick-moving cloud.

So the wind harried the sea, the sea harried the land and man who should know better harries his fellow man. A tempest of hate and violence erupts here and there — bloody outpourings that leave bruised and broken victims and death in its wake. Those who are peaceful, who live in quietness and contemplation, who carry the seeds of goodness in their hearts, walk among the violent ones seeking those who will accept and nourish the seeds and allow them to grow and flourish.

The world favours only the strong, the well-armed. Threatening voices cross the airwaves. Voices backed with the instruments of war, with the terrifying destructiveness of atomic power and deadly rockets. Such immature behaviour. They say that truth and right living must be protected by force. They forget that soon they will celebrate Christmas, in remembrance of He who lived without protection, who cared not for the length of His days on Earth but only for its spiritual quality. Such is the power of goodness and love that those who are one with it are unable to protect themselves from the ill will of their fellow men.

Each new emerging nation, on gaining independence from former colonial powers, turns first to arms and the techniques of war. They are considered of paramount importance. Many are the advanced nations prepared to supply the equipment and the necessary techniques. Where there is profit to be made, morality takes a back seat.

Hail then, the men of power, the governments of power. Those with the mightiest armies talk with the loudest voices. They move to protect the weak, to preserve the peace of the world. They fail to see that armies are the threat to peace. That without arms, trained personnel and those in charge, people could not wage war against each other. Armies serve a single purpose — to destroy and kill. For this they are trained and equipped. To this they are dedicated.

Peace cannot be protected by force. Force shatters peace and wherever it is, active peace is absent. Only a way of life, ideas and attitudes toward life can be protected. Men of peace carry their own banners. Their badge is love, their arms, understanding. Equipped with this they walk amid an alien world expressing peace, living peace and making little impression on a world that relies on war machines for self-protection.

There is no longer trust in gentler human qualities. The feel of a gun in the hand is the reassurance of security, reinforced by rocket projectiles that point skywards, jet bombers and fighters that fly the skies, bombloads ready, warships that patrol the oceans carrying offensive and destruction delivering equipment. All this to protect the nation, and the more destructive the weapons and the more organised the means, the safer a nation feels.

Why is it that people cannot live without armies and war equipment? Why is there such a lack of self-understanding, such a depth of fear creating the need for this kind of security? Why are humans, supposedly the highest form of life, unable to build a togetherness that includes everyone on the planet? Why the disjointed and separate approaches, the isolation through national, language and ethnic differences and the suspicion and antagonistic attitudes that follow?

National, religious and ideological isolation hasn't worked to produce a base for harmony and peaceful living. Yet, in spite of failure after failure through isolation, people still show no great desire for unity. We are one entity — in fact, not fancy. We've yet to realise this and so we opt for separation and all the problems and violence this brings. We put up with the consequences of isolated and separatist thinking, painful as it is and has been, and ignore the tremendous spiritual potential of which we are a part.

Must we remain blind to our true needs — the realisation of the spiritual strangeness? To those who feel the present situation should be brought to an end, who feel this must come from within and not from the present leaders, we urge you to seek a new directive to inform and guide you. The absence of this spiritual directive has meant people have placed themselves in the hands of various authorities with the permission to build a society that suits their inclinations.

This has failed to lead people to the promised land of wellbeing, economic stability and peace. Where are the truly happy people? There is insecurity, fear, persecution and violence, war here and war there. We fail miserably in the field of human relationships. Centuries of experience in living and where has it got us? Problems and troubles compound. They do not lessen.

Yet we have all we need inwardly to do so much better. We have been endowed with a wondrous nature. Turn inwards towards the Silent Heart of what we are. Listen not to the fears and concerns of the mind. Listen to the intimations of the heart. Mind leads to culs de sac of restricted living. There is no flowering through the mind, no unfolding of the highest nature. Mind will keep you trapped in time, riddled with differences, dancing to the tune of fear and self-security.

Lift yourselves out of the doldrums of the mind. The timeless is waiting for those eager and young enough to throw aside what they appear to be. Mind will hold on to what it knows, to what it has been accustomed to. It prefers to stay a cripple in time than expand into a timeless eternity. Something deep within needs to impel you there — something stronger than the mind and everything it projects.

If the inner longing is sustained, if it never flags, then in spite of mind and the tricks it gets up to, in spite of its resistance and holding on, in spite of its illusions, delusions, opinions and beliefs, the spiritual directive can step in. And then you'll learn what living in the spiritual is, what it can do for you.

Filled with the inspiration of it, mind will be cock-a-hoop with joy and feeling. It will strut and crow like a young rooster. Oh how it will shout in its excitement. Such a sense of liberation, of expansion and lightness. Where is sorrow? Gone. Where is ignorance? Gone. Where is fear? Gone. Where is everything that held us back and made living a parody, denying the human expression the enrichment of the spiritual directive? Gone. Gone. Gone.

So welcome to the spiritual those of you who have walked this way, who share its blessing. May you live forever in the bosom of its timeless nature.

❧❧

WHEN THE SOUND OF THE WATERFALL STOPPED

T HE MUSICAL SOUND of the waterfall echoed and re-echoed across the forested hills. Its noise was not the roar of a mighty torrent but the quieter rippling of a gentle cascade. Born high in the hills where the granite base permitted a rapid runoff, the many streams of running water had gradually merged as they flowed downwards, first into vigorous rivulets, then eventually into a single stream coursing down a narrow channel in the rocks that suddenly came to an end. Over this the water surged, its momentum carrying it out and down in a series of descending curves till it reached a lower level. Here it formed a small lake, its surface broken by a scattering of large boulders — rocky outcrops that would defy the erosive effects of running water for many years.

On the outer edges of the lake, tall gum trees thrust slender branches skywards. The leafy boughs filtered the light from the sun, breaking it up till only mottled reflections of shade touched the earth beneath and the nearby reaches of water. The trunks of the gums flowed strong and smooth out of the earth — immense strength built layer by layer over the years by the natural processes of a busy nature. High overhead, birds were flying from branch to branch, searching for food or chirping and calling gaily to one another. Their feathered bodies, wings flashing in flight, tails outstretched, responding beautifully to the inward desire to move, to fly, to be on the go.

Through the shaded parts of the bush, moving into the spaces between the undergrowth, a small lad, dark brown in colour, moved like an even darker shadow. He had curly black hair, a chubby face, coal-black eyes that glistened with delight in response to the natural world about him. His teeth when he laughed flashed pearl white across his dark face. His feet were bare and where he walked, hardly a ripple of impression marked the surface of the earth. The small, sturdy body was naked. He was a child of nature and not yet had the ways of civilisation touched him with its contaminating ways.

Without fear he moved towards the pool at the bottom of the waterfall and climbed onto a large boulder. From this vantage point he could watch the splash and play of the watery cascade. He sat entranced by the scene, his dark body in its stillness almost an extension of the rock he rested on. Spray glistened along the edges of the falling water. Where the light rays from the sun touched the suspended droplets, they shone pearl-like in dancing moments of delight. The musical murmur of the waterfall pervaded the area, and caressed the ears of the listening boy whose face was now set in a spontaneous contemplation.

A rapt attention slowly took over. His surface attention faded, lost in the ever growing interest that the natural surrounds effortlessly evoked in him. The Being in nature reached out and ever so gently touched the Being in the lad, caressing it till it slowly awakened and joyfully reached out to accept and entwine with that which stirred it into wakefulness. For a brief, silent moment a holy communion took place, a sudden awaking of beauty, of a deeper sensitivity. The child was lost in a contemplation vaster than space, ageless and timeless. In this split second, the sounds of the forest, of the cascading fall, formerly so distinct, ceased completely, frozen into that strange silence that alone has the power to possess in this manner.

And the child knew it not — only that delight stirred his nature into a joyous outpouring. So, chuckling in the way that happy children do, he rose, filled with a contentment that children do not analyse but accept completely, and made his way back to where he came from, untroubled and carefree, talking in friendly fashion to the birds and the trees on the way.

❧❧

NATURAL TRANQUILLITY

ONE MORNING I sat quietly in our garden on the dry, sandy earth. A fresh sea breeze stirred the leaves of the trees. Where I sat, with my back to a background of ivy leaves, I was somewhat sheltered from the wind by an apple tree and a large rosemary bush.

I dwelt in the quietness, in the peaceful presence of leafy greenness. The wind, filtering through the backdrop of trees and shrubs, flowed around my body, gently playing tug-of-war with my hair. The fresh feel of the wind was part of the surrounding tranquillity. I gazed around at each part of the garden in turn — just looked, asking no what or why of the plants or the doves walking nearby, foraging for food.

So many questions are asked of life, so many explanations offered. Life goes on unaffected by the questing mind. The green world is untroubled by questions nor does it seek answers. It is what it is, responding to the changing seasons, going through the cycle of seed, growth, fruiting, producing seed, then decay. All without complaint. Seemingly mute, it responds to sun, water and earth, acted upon by natural conditions and in turn leaving its mark on the environment.

The plant world goes its way without protest, without reaching out to be bigger or better by deliberate intent. Self-consciousness is not the way of plants. This is the world of man and with it goes dissatisfaction, torment, uncertainty and problems, the desire to expand, to be more.

Would that we could not only be self-conscious but also have the tranquillity of a tree. To be calm whatever storms come one's way would be a considerable asset. To take the buffeting then restore and repair the damage without inner loss would be commendable. This is the inner poise reflected by the sages, by those whose hearts are anchored in sublime stillness. This is a strength of a different kind, natural in its expression yet arising after years of selfless development. The weakness of ego expression has been eradicated to be replaced by spiritual strength, by what issues forth from the Eternal.

Physical strength, outstanding success in the field of sport, in various walks of life are not its immediate purpose. This may come to pass or may not. It is considered irrelevant. The sages are inwardly fixed on spiritual flowering, on dwelling in the Universal. Ego is banished, not permitted to hold centre stage of the human expression.

They live a strange life. Outwardly similar, inwardly so different. Serenely still, they stay anchored beyond thought, though outwardly active in time. The tempests of time do not rage to disturb the inner equanimity. The incoming tide is muted by love and turned away. They have a rocklike stability untouched by the fracases of time. Timeless their refuge — where they dwell. They are the timeless ones, co-joined in a loving unity with the Universal.

❧

CREATURES OF THE NIGHT – AND AWARENESS

I T'S TWILIGHT TIME and the soft shades of night are filtering through the trees, softening the landscape. A cool, light breeze hustles in from the sea and stirs the leaves into gentle movement. The sky has a soft look, here and there a star glows. Birds have gone to roost — the branches are their perches and the clusters of leaves their blanket of protection from prying eyes and the chill of the night. They nestle without fear, heads sunk low on their feathered breasts, eyes gently closed. A sense of cosy contentment pervades the scene.

Twilight fades into darkness. The stars take over the sky and the blackness of night takes over the earth. Silence spreads, broken now and then by the sound of an insect. The rhythm of nature has dropped to a gentler level and only the shy creatures of the night are abroad. Slowly, quietly they move and only the squeal of their prey disturbs the silence. Their passage through the night leaves a whispering wake heard by the sensitive ears attuned to the right pitch.

They are the creatures of darkness and not to be seen by the eyes of the day. They are at home in the inky shadows where they wait unseen with senses alert for the prey that life may bring their way. They feed on the warm flesh and blood of those who are their kin and little they care, for they too must live. Hunger knows no love, only a torment that must be appeased. They go their way through the night and live out life's plan for their kind, content to do so, for instinct and their kind of intelligence seeks nothing else.

Yet in their way they express a capacity to live life as fully as their form and endowed characteristics allow. Even if there is danger to be faced there is also the joy of play with their kind, of courtship and a busy life to be lived under the stars. And when death calls to collect its due as sometime it must, they go and take their cherished impressions with them. No more then will they nuzzle each other or wait for tasty food to come their way. The soft eyes that gathered light from stars or moon will no longer see, nor will the sensitive tide of life drift through, directing them to live, play and mate.

On nature's rubble heap of unused material they will be cast to decompose until such time as transformation incorporates the remains so completely into the earth that little evidence remains of what was once so active. The marvellous images that fused into the creature's experience of itself and the outer world will have faded into a seeming nothingness.

What wonderful natural processes made this possible? Do eyes create what they see or do they merely observe what has been fashioned for them to see? Does the brain create images or does it only register that they are there? Why do we receive the outside world as our own appearance and images? Do we rely solely on the brain and sense organs to apprehend what we know? Or have these sensitive recording instruments been fashioned to receive what is creatively presented by a remarkable sensitivity? What lights up the brain, making seeing, hearing and feeling possible? What puts sense into us so that we understand the world we live in? Is it only an arrangement of flesh or something entirely different?

The sensitivity that records the moving panorama of life is surely a separate principle. It can never be separate from its universal source however much it animates the body and identifies with it. We are this sensitivity, this awareness. Although cast in flesh for a time and seduced by the senses into accepting the form as the all, awareness remains as it is — the light by which we live and know. This is the unchanging nature we are, regardless of the changing face of time, having no identifiable image in what we are, in our true nature.

∽✦∽

DESERT INTERLUDE

THE DESERT VOICE speaks out with scorching heat and sandy wastes, with singing winds and drifting sand, with blistering hot rocks and burning sun. Her voice is the dunes that run before the wind, the towering cactus that thrives, sending strange arms upwards, begging; the desert mouse that moves timidly, in search of food; the fierce rattlesnake that watches and waits with fixed eyes, body still, for the mouse to wander within striking range; the lizard that scurries restlessly onwards, looking, searching, urging for food to appease its hunger. These are all her children, all a part of her being.

None does she favour too much, none too little. Here in the dry desert arena, they live, play, hunt for food and produce their offspring. The desert surrounds are burned deep into their nature, assimilated and accepted as home, as a mode of life. They love the hot desert sand they burrow into or make their way over and the strange towering plants that throw little shafts of cooling shadows across the burning wastes. The nooks and crannies between the rocks that form a playground when dusk has fallen and the heat has lessened, these too they know and love. And, in passing on, as they fall by life's wayside as inevitably they must, with every longing beat of their being they try, desperately, to hold to that which they have known so well; urging to hold to the form, to scurry over the sands once more and feel the desert sun beat down, to warm their bodies as it had done in the past.

Vain indeed are their deep-held longings. Death is merciless and gives no time to stay but takes when it will. Such is the law of conscious life — that all forms appear as if for a moment, be what they are for that moment, then depart, to be gathered by that which is a repository for all. But creative nature takes care of its own. Replacements have been fashioned, to go forth in active form to enjoy life in the customary manner.

Such is the way of life. To give, briefly, and then to take away again. All share in her being and in sharing, come to know what it is to be, whether it be as the lizard that scuttles swiftly over sand, the snake that silently slides or the other creatures that love the desert dryness.

ۼۑ

SUDDEN DEATH

A GREY MIST writhed slowly like a sluggish serpent over the glasslike surface of the lake. Long tentacles of misty vapour curled around the paperbark trees and into the thick rushes around the lake's edges. Soft patches of mist enveloped the reeds, spread across intervening spaces of water, covering groups of drifting ducks and their tiny young. Frogs croaked and now and again the call of a water bird echoed across the lake, penetrating the mist with strident suddenness.

The water, lapping against the reeds, swayed them into gentle movement. Ripples, caused by lightly falling rain, patterned the surface with widening circles of movement. Raindrops splashing into the lake broke into droplets of sound. Ducks preened their feathers as their young huddled in closer. Damp the atmosphere, yet with a snug cosiness about it. The water birds were one with the drifting water. They rose and fell in rhythm with its motion.

Then suddenly, unexpected commotion. From the reed-covered shore, a duck broke out of cover, wings flapping furiously, an alarm call flung from its throat. Impelled by fear, it moved fast and high. The explosive crack of a rifle shot shattered the harmony and a split second later a bullet shattered the body of the duck. It fell, a crumpled, broken thing, to the water below where it floated limply on the surface.

The hunter, from his shelter in the reeds, lowered his rifle, a smile of satisfaction on his face. The excitement of the kill was still alive in him. For the duck he had no compassion, no feeling of sadness. Were they not here to be killed for his pleasure, so he could experience the exultation his skill with a rifle could bring? Patiently he had crouched, waiting for the opportune moment. The flash of the flying duck, the swift sweep of the following rifle, the squeeze of the trigger and the loud retort — these were all over now. So was the life of the duck.

The hunter packed his gun away and left the scene. The body of the victim rolled with the lapping water. Gently caressed by its motion, the duck drifted without feeling. It swirled here and there, a disjointed, lifeless thing. Neck, wings and legs moved limply to and fro. Gone — gone was the duck. No more would its gay quacking be heard across the lake. No more would it nestle with its young. It had rejoined the timeless source of life, there to rest where no hunter could ever reach it again.

❧❧

UNTOUCHED BY DEATH

W HY HAS THE grave become symbolic of the melancholy end of our life's aspirations? An upright stone block, name, age, relationship inscribed in brief detail, a grassed over plot of ground or a solid, stone covering — this invokes disturbing feelings of how transient life is and how soon the vitality and richness of its expression are over. With death we will no longer enjoy the magic of life in this colourful garden of timeful experience we love so much.

The silent face of death is so different from the smiling face of active life. So too is the smooth, fresh face of a child from the lined and wrinkled face of old age. The young in nature begin life in much the same way. Resilient, pliable, tender and supple with healthy colour and full of energetic go-go-go. Life bursts into eager activity in the young stages of its expression. It pours its vitality, its urge to grow and expand into the development of its living forms.

Energy, interest and enthusiasm to explore flow constantly out of children. No inward looking of any consequence, no troublesome questioning about the what and why of life — just involvement with others and the outer world. Such is the restless drive of the very young. Flowing action that has little deeper meaning to children and they make of living experience a playground into which they direct their youthful energy with exuberance and constant chattering. They do not ask more of the adult world than they be allowed to do this without undue interference and surrounded by loving protection.

With old age the process reverses itself somewhat. Interest in the outer wanes and older people find they cannot be bothered doing things in which they were formerly so actively engaged. What was so important in their young time has lost some of its lustre. They are inclined to be introspective, musing often on the meaning of life, and they begin to look closer at the end called death as its calling card begins to edge its corner into their lives. First, with the thoughts that they are getting older and slower. Then as more years pass the acknowledgment settles in that any day soon, any moment, the card may be presented and there is no other option but to accept it and go with death wherever it may take them.

Older people tend to drift back in time via the dreamlike path of memory, reminiscing often and looking with a resignation that acknowledges the difference. Memory reminds them of when their world was so very young and fresh and they too were part of that freshness, gazing with wide-eyed innocence at the world about. How eagerly surroundings were explored then. Childish enthusiasm knew no bounds except those imposed by parents and older people. Under the protective mantle of parents' love the young surge into action, like ocean waves racing shoreward, driven by the irresistible winds of curiosity to gambol and taste the experiences in the garden of time.

Living, growing up and settling into society absorb the attention early. Childhood years, teenage years, then into marriage and raising children. We are on an express train in time and the scenery flashes past. There is barely time to notice the wonder of life's flowing movement. Gradually the train begins to slow down, going slower and slower, till it comes to the final standstill of death. Then the body rapidly decays, breaking down into crumbling bones and dust that have no resemblance to the fleshly form that paraded down life's highway, head held high, eyes sparkling, eager voice chattering. Here it had tasted to the full the heady wine of experiences that beckoned so invitingly.

We are somewhat chastened by the death of those we know well. The impact is saddening. At the funeral, the lamentations, the heartbreaking cries, the tears that flow from sorrow-filled eyes, the black mourning clothes, make for a sombre and depressing occasion. So much so, that if one is not too involved with the family of the deceased there is relief in leaving the service and going somewhere else, perhaps down to the beach to be alone for a time, to see the sights and hear the sounds of nature unruffled by the disturbances that affect the mind. Here, where waves flow over the sandy shore, we leave clear imprints of our feet on the wet sand as we walk.

The sound of the waves gently breaking, like glass shattering in slow motion, is so soothing in comparison to the lamentations left behind. The sun warmly shines and the gulls rest on the beach, dreaming in the wind, or fly slowly above, and here in this serenity, impressions of death fade, for the mind does not wish to linger on that which is painful.

The young, for a time, have the capacity to fight against downhill travel in life. They urge to surge upward and resist decay. But they too eventually succumb to the effects of time and gradually withdraw into a narrower circle of endeavour, buffeted by the wear and tear of life into taking a place in the wings rather than standing central stage where the spotlight of youthful achievement shone so brightly.

Can humans do no better than this? Must we succumb to decay and death? Are these deadly two invincible? Isn't there anything in the human expression that resists the intentions of this relentless duo from having their way with us? Are we fated to succumb and sink without a trace when the hand of death strikes, decaying our exterior form and doing we know not what to our inner self? The body must decay, this is acknowledged. The mind loses its steady contact with the world it knew. Communication ceases with those it formerly held in earnest conversation. This too is known.

But there is a lingering hope buried deep in the hearts of many that living has not been in vain and that something in us survives, to rise phoenix-like above death. Something untouched, undecaying, and that once more they will walk, talk and share some kind of communication with others much as they formerly did. So humans fashion an image of the hereafter out of this hope and project a heaven where they can roam again, including in this image, if they are religious, a god of some kind with whom to share this heaven.

Is this personality we know worthy of eternal survival? Or do we desire it so because we are so fond of and completely identified with this showy aspect of our nature; and knowing no other and being afraid of non-existence, want to perpetuate the self in its familiar form because this is all we believe ourselves to be? The self cannot bear to be alone. It extends itself through relationships with family, friends and surroundings.

Even in death relatives strive to maintain the link. Tombstones, monuments, memorials to the dead have name, date and detail engraved on them to remind the world of those who once lived. Such a sad reaching out to maintain ties with a past that is over. Yet in spite of the elaborate send-offs for the departed, those who remain still long for something death cannot touch. Does anything eternal really exist? And have we any connection with it? What we see and know of ourselves, we expect to die. Experience is transitory. Every moment of time passes and we along with it. Is there, then, nothing in us that time cannot change, corrupt or destroy?

The answer to this lies not in time where all decays, even the bursting promise of springtime that blossoms into overwhelming growth, young and pliant, only to drift into the fading colours of autumn and the cold sleep of winter. Not in the thoughts and reasons of the mind that rise and fall like the tides of the sea and jump every which way like grasshoppers, changing from one standpoint to another; but in the Universal side to our nature, in Being rather than becoming. Becoming is change, birth and death. Being is changeless. In this there is not action, nor living centres, neither birth nor death. This is the serene, not the agitated, the essence of stillness, of life not created, of movement not put into motion, of existence devoid of chattering creatures.

Death and decay cannot touch it. There are no forces to bring about death. There is only a strangeness that does not permit any disturbance to its pristine nature. Journey there if you will and you will find your own answer to death and to life, not in words but in discovery, and in so doing you will meet that which has been referred to as the creator of all things.

But do not expect to understand its nature in the ways the mind normally understands. It exists and it is enough that humans can share it through revelation. The difference it makes to living will astound you, even confound you, and all we can do about it is accept it, like we do our birth, our living and our death.

TOWARD DISCOVERY

N OWADAYS, PEOPLE DO not smile as often and as warmly as they once did. They seem more uncertain and the confidence reflected at the time of the economic boom of the late 1960s and early 1970s has faded. Before the tragedy of World War 2, people were somewhat closer and the appreciation of life, of the little things they did, day after day, was deeper, even though there was less money and nothing like the extensive range of goods we have to choose from today.

Now shops, stores and saleyards are packed with an abundance of food, gadgets, furniture, electrical devices, cars and knick-knacks with enough variety to satisfy any demand, appetite or desire. Such an array, beautifully packaged, attractively presented, with the advertising accent on buy for any reason whatsoever.

And the constant changes. Innovation running riot as the mind's genius for invention continues with accelerating momentum. The hectic pace proceeds in every direction at breakneck speed. New developments, even with the economic downturn, show little sign of abating and the mood is still go-go-go in every which way we please. Yet still, in spite of this material abundance there is a growing undercurrent of concern in dealing with the changes so the enjoyment of life deepens.

With the climbing demands and pressures of modern living we seem to be losing our grip somewhat as uncertainty grows as to where we are going. Expectations have changed as to what we should have and do and people now strive to extract a greater reward from living and working. This intention to make of life a grand supplier that meets our deepest needs affects every social aspect, and education and productive energy are directed towards satisfying demands and desires in the determined directions.

In this, the mind is the controlling factor that intends to lead humanity to peaceful living, happiness and a plentiful supply of what is needed or desired. Through work, education and inclination, what then are people after in life? Certainly they seek a continuation of life and in this the production of food is necessary. Comfort too is desirable, so we build our shelters, manufacture clothing, furniture for our homes and a range of gadgets for our personal needs.

Pain, we intend to avoid. The afflictions of the body we leave to the medical profession but we do take care to avoid sickness and injury in the way we live. But paradoxically, while people desire to avoid pain they will often indulge in habits that bring this into their lives.

Happiness and enjoyment are other expectations we have. This is variable, each person having different ideas as to what this means. Certainly, there is an extensive movement by the discerning to fashion lifestyles that please, and choosing from the social offerings on display is an important part of this enjoyment.

Satisfaction and achievement are also sought as worthwhile ends, bringing not only outer rewards but boosting self-worth inwardly. They are somewhat interrelated and again they are variables. What deeply satisfies some is of no interest at all to others. Education as a means of self-return is also sought after by many. Basically there are two kinds. One that supplies the skills to be put to social use and through which money is earned to provide the necessities of living; the other often purely an interest, something to be involved in such as arts, crafts, painting, although these too can be turned to earning money if so desired.

In this kind of education people apply themselves to further their learning in directions they may not be able to put to monetary use. They may study ancient history, archaeology, gain a background in science, politics, religion or social studies, embracing other nations though they may never travel. Education for the sake of learning is expanding and it supplies inner satisfaction to those involved. In spite of what education and the variety in living offers today, humans are still restless and dissatisfied and demand something more from life.

Education is accepted as the gateway to this something more. It is expected to yield a sense of ultimate achievement and begins with a setting of targets, then work and application till the desired end is attained. This suffices till the immediate objectives are realised, then another target is set and humans are off again on the trail to further achievements.

Expansion of the self through education is what the self seeks. There is often dissatisfaction with life, with the level of intelligence, with the lack of knowledge, with the fitness or appearance of the body, the work we do, even with possessions after they lose their initial newness.

People will move in new fields to counter this. We will work like beavers to improve ourselves, to change through ideas, to gain social approval or just because we want to be better. The self we are may not be acceptable in our own eyes or in the sight of others, so it must be nurtured by achievement, practice, intention, work and education until it becomes greater, better than the raw material nature brought into being.

Experience provides the stepping stones travelled in the urge for self-improvement. Without experience, learning is stunted. They are divided into those with more value and those with less. Those who expand the vision of self-growth are vigorously pursued. As long as the self is convinced the value is there it will continue to pursue those avenues that reassure it in its commitment to self-enhancement. It will gravitate towards the experiences, determined by itself or suggested by others, that meet with its approval and from which it expects to gain the greatest benefit.

It is an extensive reaching out that the self is involved in, searching perhaps for self-fulfilment so it gains a sense of having done something worthwhile with its life and not just lived it mechanically from day to day in boring routines that do not offer much in value.

Does the self ever pause from its extensive involvement and ask what self-fulfilment means? Whether through achievement it can lift itself, in a real sense, out of the lower bracket of self-worth it has placed itself in into an upper one of higher importance merely by the accumulation of experience, education or achieving a different role in life? Or does it remain throughout essentially what it is?

It is the motives behind the action the self should be clear on, not the actual doing, for it is going to continue in some kind of direction for whatever purpose. It will not sit being inactive for long. If the purpose behind its motivations is just to expand in self-importance, then it should look into this to understand the implications behind its actions. The expansion may be only in its own eyes or by measures imposed by social standards and judgments, whereas there may be no shift in the basic value of what essentially a human being is, even though society may place greater worth on the end result.

We have little appreciation of what we are in essence and we hold to the idea that only through what we do, achieve or acquire do we gain in value and social standing. And this gives us security and satisfaction, which are supports we crave or need in our movement through life. Can the nature of the self be basically changed then, or is it its expression that is altered, which is an entirely different matter? Does the self become greater, more important through what it does, or does it just rearrange its experiences? There is a distinction between basic nature and expression.

We cannot deny certain experiences and actions we express please us greatly, or that we will avoid others at all cost. But what is the true nature of the self we are, before we achieve, after or at any time in between? And does this vary as the outer varies?

In the haste to impel itself outwards into achievement, into self-growth through effort, the mind rarely dwells on this reflectively. It prefers to base its conclusions on appearance, ideas and judgments based on social standards rather than on the actuality of what it is. Because the mind does not explore its nature inwardly, it drives itself into outer expansion, expecting by doing so it will gain in value inwardly.

Why then does it feel of lesser value without a greater standing in the community? Has it not the same capacity to express the human capacity regardless of its role in life? Once a certain level of education is acquired or a vocation with greater responsibility, does the sensitive appreciation of life change? Does this change the quality of awareness of our surroundings, the depth of our feeling towards others and the environment or the range of qualities we reflect?

We may reason in this way but will still insist in coming to ground in some type of activity, achievement or experiences that will supply us the sense of value we do not seem to have, and which we expect to create via the avenues in which we indulge.

The motives that drive the self onwards to the security and reassurance it craves will only come to rest when it has come face to face with what it is behind the facades it wears. This is a nature not given to explanations, dissection; nor can it be used as a springboard towards achievement. It is a nature in which values such as high or low do not apply.

When the reality is realised, the self learns distinction is only on the surface. This deeper nature will remain as it is, neither expanded nor diminished by what the self does. It will remain perfect and complete, a mystery that cannot be violated by intrusion.

The value that was formerly missing is now there by divine decree and the self hasn't any need to make of itself something different to please itself or others. It shares a value higher by far than any the mind can devise as it journeys its social surrounds where delusions of greatness and self-importance parade their facades of spurious worth; reflecting a counterfeit value that is avidly sought by those who have not journeyed inwards and thereby do not know the difference between the true and the false in these things.

Do then what you must in the way of needs, desire and interest. Direct your deepest aspirations, your most earnest intentions and your greatest interest not toward social security, individual expansion or the variety life has to offer, but toward discovery. For in this is a treasure trove of values in ways you can never evaluate until you discover the strangeness that you are.

And in discovery, life reveals a meaning the mind can never give to it. Although what presents itself as such is way beyond our measure of understanding, yet it brings to living a richness and a warmth, peace and contentment, an overflowing thankfulness to be a part of it. Also, a depth of understanding that makes living and sharing much more enjoyable. As humans, could we ask any more of life?

❧

BEYOND RITUAL

WE WORSHIP THE form. We revere the face. We repeat the sacred word. We honour the ritual. Yet we seek the Great Stillness, the Silence beyond form, sound or ritual. We live in the outer, dwell in rituals, utter the word, sing sacred songs, and listen to divine music. So we fill our lives with meaning. Stillness and Silence pass us by.

Because our lives are bereft of the Silence we do not know, we create our own — the silence of body and thought — or find a quiet spot where plants grow. In this we dwell.

But mind is ever restless and ego is its twin. There are things to do and the body must move sometime. The world of mind and body covers the Great Stillness. The images in the mirror of time take over — of sensation and success, of failure and fun, of everything we know as life.

Mind turns itself inside out looking for the Great Stillness. Wherever it goes, whatever it does, the noise of the mind is there. Stillness is shy. It hides from the busy mind. It abides in silence. Mind prefers its own kind — being in movement, being involved, doing this, doing that, practising — all the things that mind can do. Mind is steeped in separation, in contrasts; in 'I am this, you are that', in differentiation. This flows out of the mind.

Stillness is all embracing, all loving. 'All is One' is its theme. It abhors separation, the lesser and the greater, the contrasts of the mind. It melts all this away, the sense of being mind and body too.

Unexpectedly, it catches the mind by surprise. When mind drops its guard for a moment, it slips in uninvited and takes over. Who can explain it, who can tell you why? It happens and when it does, astonishment follows, or laughter, or joy.

Mind performs cartwheels of movement in its search, works hard at projecting its own idea of stillness, busies itself with this and that. The cyclone of time, that's what it is. Tell me what to do. Show me the way. Give me a path to travel along adorned with pleasant scenery. Let me hold a guru's hand. Let me do something. Nothing worthwhile comes to the mind without action from the self. So determines the mind.

Stillness waits for the mind to slip into self-forgetfulness, for the mind to tire, to give over and step aside for a moment. Not by deliberate intent this. Then it shows itself. It's unbelievably simple. What we know — appearance and action — immediately vanishes. For a moment Stillness takes over. That's all there is. We are 'That'. 'That' is what we are.

And we thought we were body, or something called mind, or thought, something contained, wrapped in knowledge, in a fancy package labelled 'me'. You cannot name what I am, cannot think of it, cannot apprehend it while mind dwells in movement.

In Stillness I am. No. In Stillness I am not. There is only Stillness, complete, original. Mind, go jump in the lake of self-forgetfulness. I've lived with you but there are moments I've lived without you.

And those moments of Stillness when mind is not as the actor and Silence reigns supreme are the most blessed of all. They bring what we acknowledge as peace, contentment, love, understanding, happy living, lightness of being. Mind, what more could you want? What more?

❧

A CHANCE MEETING

I MET A child who was confined to a wheelchair and the meeting stirred me deeply. I couldn't do what I wanted to do — reach out and take that child's hand and run along and play and skip together. I wanted to talk to the child and hear childish chatter in return, for such things delight the human heart. But that wasn't possible either for she couldn't hold a conversation. She could only make sounds.

To see such afflictions in humans is very distressing. Life is oft times difficult enough without such things happening and to hear it is God's will, or Karma as the Buddhists say, doesn't help much at all. Particularly to those who cope with this situation, day in and day out, giving so much of their time, love, courage and patience in looking after an afflicted person.

We question deeply the meaning of life at such times. Why should some be doomed to a very limited expression of life while others roam free doing what they will? There are people who waste their lives in so many ways. Who grow up to reflect behaviour that is displeasing, who prey on fellow humans to feed a bizarre appetite for the sensual, who live selfish lives that revolve around violence — yet they are physically well if somewhat mentally unstable.

So there is something that rankles deeply to see the sweetness of a child imprisoned in the restrictions of physical and mental disabilities and doomed to stay that way because present knowledge isn't advanced enough to effect a marked improvement.

Inner protests do not help. Life doesn't yield reasons for what it brings — at least, not reasons that satisfy and lead to calm acceptance. People acknowledge and face up to the reality of the situation because they must, because those who are strong in love and compassion will not turn away and pass the challenge over to another.

Yet humans are like reeds in the wind. They bend before pain and overload. They are buffeted mentally, physically and emotionally and they cry out for rest and peace, for a break from this heavy load that is sometimes too much to bear — too demanding to deal with.

Where there are friends also moved by love, the load is shared and life is a little less wearing. But where can one go to carry the inner burden, the frustrations, the tiredness, the tormented thinking, the longing to live as others do and share life with a child in a carefree, happy way, forging a close, open relationship in the process? All this and more must be borne by the person who carries the greater part of the overload, the mental and the emotional difficulties that arise.

Would the spiritual side of life help in such circumstances? Would it yield more of energy, love and any other qualities that would ease the difficulties? Such questions are probably asked time and again as people turn to God for help. But somehow even in a world filled with so many people we are essentially alone with our resources, our weaknesses and whatever strength we have.

Being surrounded with loving help minimises the difficulties. But we still have to live with the heartaches, with our frustrations, moods, actions and reactions whatever these are. This cannot be avoided and it is from within we need to find the courage, the understanding and the release from mounting concerns to carry on.

From this we somehow need to draw on something deeper than the mind we know, on something called the Universal, God or the spiritual so humans are supported by a greater strength, love and understanding than that with which they are normally endowed. It would be better if this did happen. Then we would have tremendous inner support as well as outer support from people and social services.

But whichever way it goes, people will carry on and some will shake their heads in sorrow at how unyielding life can be and still wonder — "Why me? Why my child?" And life will still refuse to answer.

కోుకో

THE UNWELCOME INTRUSION

P AIN — WHO HASN'T experienced it at some time in life? And doesn't it drive us to distraction? When it's with us it becomes the unwelcome focus of attention. If it's bad, we are off to the doctor, dentist or a specialist for diagnosis.

Pain, concerns and troubles are the human lot in life. Physical pain often needs medical attention. Sometimes this means more pain, an operation or various painful treatments.

What an awakener pain is and a sudden stopper of the former way of living. No way can we swing down life's highway in a free and easy manner when pain is abroad. How difficult to get relief when it's constant. The groans and moans break out, restless movements too. We try this, try that. Oh dear, what a nuisance pain is. It drives all the fun out of life.

In quieter moments of contemplation we see it brings hard lessons in learning about the self. Pain is life's unwelcome gift to the human race. Who wants that kind of gift? No one. There are no beg pardons from life, however. No 'do you mind if pain drops in for a while?' No way — just bang and it's there, right in the middle of life. Watch the reaction now. First — what's this? Then, how to get rid of it — fast.

The aim of the self? To get back on track, back to life without painful disturbance. Even if one sees the need for learning that brought it, when the lesson is learnt there is still the urgent demand to put pain aside and get back to familiar and comfortable routines. The self doesn't want to shift away from the life it knows. It wants to go back to doing its own thing — the self way.

Well, what else can it do? Desire, demand, need, choice, intention, combine to fashion the self's movement in life. Pain comes and everything stops if it's bad enough. Pain over, rehabilitation if necessary, then back to the same niche in life or as close to it as possible.

The self cuts its own groove in life. It's extensive, complex, variable, but the self wants control — the master of the human boat until it comes to grief on the shoals of pain. So, having learnt each lesson as it arises, what then? Without a new directive in life, the self can't be any different. The new has to open out and call the self away from the old ways. And the self has to be responsive, see the need to go and leave the past behind.

But the new must open out and it must be clear or the self cannot respond. Pain, as a stopper, is acknowledged. But if that's all that comes out of it, it's only part of the story. The next chapter is yet to be written. What is being asked of me? The self cannot stand still for long. When rest and recuperation are over, it's time to stir into action again.

Do I go back to the former ways that were my means of self-expression? Surely I will unless something new opens out. Pain or no pain, that's the way it is. So, over to whatever guides my direction in life.

Is it really a matter of a new direction? Or just a shift in understanding — a release of an inner build-up that re-established the self and denied the Sunshine of Life a clear outlet?

Is life unconcerned about the little things we do with our lives, or does she want her human children to be happy in the warmth of her loving protection?

Pain and disruption are the signals. The self is out of kilter with life, with the spiritual. It is time to back off from the entrapment of the self and return to the simplicity of the spiritual.

❧❧

THE DESIRE FOR PEACE

THERE IS SOMETHING deeply touching about the human longing for peace and cause for sadness in the different ways they go about realising it. This signifies a lack of understanding of the nature of the mind, of the worth of ideas, of the nature of reality and how it expresses its nature through the individual.

Those who live in the prison of the mind and know not that they do are content to stay within its confines and live accordingly. Not for them the sudden surprise of open prison gates, of the wide expanse of the Sunshine of Being beyond the prison — the sparkle of a springtime mood and the fresh stirrings of the winds of understanding from beyond the vale of time.

They live in time's beleaguered field, assailed from all directions, disturbed inwardly and outwardly by demand and response, by tempest and movement. Not for them the calmness of Silent Being — of that stillness that calms the restless mind and brings peace, where formerly conflict reigned supreme.

The glimmer of an idea stirs on the horizon of the mind. It takes up the thought, the name of peace. From within its prison darkness, it projects a ray of light to travel along. It will follow this self-created light till it comes to the journey's end of peace, then blissfully bask in its presence and enjoy the blessing it brings.

But the light way is created by the mind. It will not lead to peace in spite of the mind's good intentions. How can it when the mind has failed to understand the causes within itself that deny peace its chance to be? Peace does not lie at the end of a long trail of human initiatives like a prize to be won in return for effort expended.

The reality of what brings peace is here and now. It lies beyond the mind, beyond its concepts and ideas, beyond the scope of its imagination. When the mind is still, like a day devoid of breeze and not even a leaf of mind-created movement stirs to disrupt the tranquillity of Being, then that strange nature that is the basis of the universal expression arises to bless the human expression with its presence. And it brings with its coming that sought after longing referred to as peace. Nothing else makes true peace possible.

The tracks of the mind lead only to the illusion of peace. They have no enduring basis. The foundations are riddled with weaknesses and the formulated structures will collapse at the slightest stress. Whereas the peace that grows from within, that flows from the deepening of understanding, will endure as long as the true measure of understanding endures.

These go hand in hand in human nature. There is not the one without the other. Both flow, as a consequence, from that strange meeting between the Divine Universal and that within the human that is of the very same nature. When these meet in a timeless union that defies human understanding, a fresh inspiration arises and begins a new expression in time. One that sensitively reflects among its qualities that which is acknowledged as peace.

❧❧

A REFLECTION ON PEACE

ISN'T IT GREAT to be connected to something as important and widespread as a movement for peace? Being involved yields a sense of doing something important and worthwhile. But pause a little and reflect on the why and wherefore of this involvement, of the intentions behind it.

A deliberate intention to bring peace into the world — organising and working for something that is lacking in life. Why is this so? The word peace has such a lovely sound. It rolls off the tongue as easily as humans should be expressing this tranquil state that signifies the absence of strife, violence and warfare.

Where peace reigns in the human heart, there is joy and happiness in being alive, in being together, in sharing the human expression. Being at peace means humans have come to rest in the heartland of the highest value of all.

Not by deliberate intention, nor by organisation of the mind for any purpose, by mutual agreement, declaration or otherwise, can peace arise on noble wings and lay to rest the stubborn, persistent flow of conflict that emanates from the human mind. And stay, to benefit the human race with its gentle qualities.

It is not born of the mind, that tempest of reaction, the breeding ground of contention. Rather, it comes in the wake of a fresh understanding, from something completely new, not connected with the mind's endeavours.

At that strange meeting when the Universal draws the human into its fold, a great love stirs to touch that side of human nature that has never known peace, which is like a desert, barren of the sweet flow of the essence of life.

Taking part in peace parades signifies the mind's intentions. But without giving over its background, without yielding its divided social and individual standing in full understanding of so doing, its intentions will falter and it will be back where it started.

And there is too, the danger of self-delusion. Humans cannot stay as they are, not change inwardly and expect peace to follow as a consequence. This is the difficult part on the way to peace. All else is easy in comparison.

True change is brought about by discovery, by contact with the Divine. It begins not on the surface by declaration, nor even by human intention, but in those strange moments when the Divine reveals its nature and the individual centre of contention fades away and momentarily does not exist with its trouble breeding ways.

Out of this meeting is born the beginning of a new expression. If it continues, so the new will strengthen. And if it stays, so too will peace become a reality without effort on our part. And those touched by the Divine shall know what it means to live when the heart is full and the mind is no longer the dominant factor in the human expression. May peace claim us all.

❧

HARMONY IS POSSIBLE

T HE NATURAL ORDER, if left to itself, proceeds in the accustomed way. Plants grow and die, life gives birth to life, the seasons come and go and everything fits into place.

How different the contentious world of humans who differ over just about everything. We argue every step of the way, about development, social arrangements, religions, what to do and how to do it. Not for us an orderly progression but rather we grind and grate against each other — self jostling self for supremacy.

In the process we organise, gathering together those who think likewise, who want much the same things. Organisations give more power, more control to people to have their own way. How much simpler, in a way, is the natural order. Everything doing what it must, without resistance — acted through so the overall continuity of life and surroundings proceeds with its own kind of harmony.

Is it possible for humans to proceed with uninterrupted harmony and come together to make unanimous decisions all are happy with? Not bloody likely. Not without an all-in brawl if the issues dealt with are deeply divisive. In such cases, solutions are hammered out at the end of a bruising session of exhausting give and take discussions. And if the divisions go deep enough, and a solution is not forthcoming, why then, a war is the means to settle the matter.

Why all this bruising and battering just to live together? We all want to be happy, don't we? We do not want pain or disturbance to interfere with our enjoyment. We want a lifestyle of our choosing, not to be hurt or hurt others. Yet this is what happens when we come together in social living.

So, what is wrong with us? Did we miss out in our development? Did nature look after everything else but not the human race, leaving us somehow incomplete and unable to live together without friction developing? Is it our fault in ways we do not understand because we ignore our creative potential for harmony, for living as a unified people from the highest level of our spiritual existence?

Perhaps, unlike animals and plants, living does not come easy for us. They do not have to make a deliberate attempt to learn as we do. Their living just follows as a natural consequence but for humans it is different and often difficult. We grope our way forward learning from mistakes, costly mistakes at times.

And were it not for the very special learning offered through enlightened intermediaries between God and the human race, we would not be aware there exists the opportunity for a different kind of living. One based on one-ness, not separation. Realise this, act on it, and then see what harmony flows in day to day living.

&

ON LIGHT, MIND AND THE WORLD

THE OUTER WORLD is an extension of our universal nature. Both the individual and the world are born of the one creative process. The individual knows itself through the world and the world is brought into being known by the light of awareness. Both are given meaning and reality by the nature of awareness, which is the basis, the existence of all things.

Awareness shines and the world comes to life — into existence out of what appears to be the darkness of non-existence. The darkness of non-existence is our own projection, born of the mind's division of perception. We divide into life and not life — into life and death, into being and not being, into mind and matter, into self and the non-self.

We impose our perceptions, our illusions on the self and the world. Both become, in our eyes, what we say they are. We call ourselves body and mind and the world, matter and energy. This conclusion is born of our perceptions, of a sense-based view of outer phenomena. The senses dictate their vision of things by their very structure. By the manner of their design and function the senses report a particular picture of the self and the world to the observing mind. They report what they are designed to report, see what they must see, feel what they must feel, hear what they must hear.

Through the senses we give birth to the whole range of our experience of the self and the world. Through the sensitivity we are, the individual, the senses and the known world come into being. Sensitivity is primary, is the magic that kindles the lesser light of the self into existence. The sensitivity never loses touch with the self or the outside world. In reality, it never changes its fundamental nature, but by projection and the nature of experience, the illusion is created of many. This covers the light of the sensitivity.

The mind lives in the many, the mind lives in the One. The One lives in and is the very nature of the mind. When we see and say that only difference is real, that is the illusion of the unilluminated mind — of a mind living without the One Light. When this light is absent, the mind sees many lights, many shades, even darkness. It sees sorrow and pain, beginning and end, justice and injustice — all the polarities.

The mind that grows back into the One Light sees the world of appearance, is absorbed in its wonder but sees also something else. It sees only one nature, the source of all things, the source of all experience. All eyes are the eyes of this nature, of this sensitivity. Through the self it is this light that looks out on the world that is its own creation. By so doing, it loses the knowledge of its own nature. It observes the flesh and blood image (the physical body) cast in time and space; and such is the ethereal nature of the light and so overwhelming the nature of appearance that to the unilluminated, the appearance dominates as the only reality — as all that exists.

The light is covered by appearance. The mind lives and plays in the world of appearance, is drawn towards the outer show, seeks its sustenance here, depends on this and loses itself in the process. Lost in time, the mind slowly withers, decays and sees death as the end. Severed from the vine of life by its own intransigence, it slowly starves. Denied the inner richness of life it turns toward the riches it creates by its own hand and holds fast to these. Its holdings in time become its values, measured in terms of rituals, social arrangements for living, possessions according to kind — all now the foundations on which the mind builds its edifice of security and its meaning for living.

It lives now in the outer show, in the arrangements, and when it moves, or tries to give a higher meaning to life by searching for the One Light, it clutters up its movement by the dead weight of its adopted approach, with set ideas on how it should proceed. It does not move lightly, uncluttered by experience, without an overload of complications. To the mind it seems an impossibility to move towards something worthwhile without a security backup of some kind, without the reassurance of rituals, without actions initiated by itself.

Yet, how can it realise the One Light by keeping to the pathways of time and effort? When will its search come to an end? It moves always onward, looking for a rainbow's end, at the end of a ritual road, meditational movement, or reasonable reflection. Always mind on the move extending itself. Where is the One Light in this?

It is the mind's illusion that it is separate from the One Light, a spell cast by the senses impressing the mind with reports of separation.

As it moves from place to place in the outer, so it expects to move on the inner. It cannot be still, not for a moment. It tries, but its stillness is mind induced — by self-intention. It is the stillness of the seeker, of that which is searching for the One Light.

What is the nature of that which searches? Is it different in nature from that which it seeks? In time, as the self, it weaves a web of descriptions and complications. I call it the 'chatter-bug of time'. It's never still — always filling life with its own noise, searching, reaching out, longing for something. With all this commotion, the One Light cannot be realised. That's why a natural stillness is so important. Not mind induced, nor arranged.

When this natural stillness arises, the One Light is there. All the commotion of a self in motion has come to a momentary end. So too, has the search. The mind and the One Light have come together in a timeless blend. They never were apart, never separated except by thought.

∾

ON MATTERS SPIRITUAL

S OCIETY IS STILL rather shy when it comes to discussion or reference to the spiritual aspects of mankind's existence. Even though there is a much wider awareness now and there are far more books, magazines, seminars, public talks that encourage interest on the subject of our spiritual connection with the Universal Nature, yet still it is not something that finds ready acceptance wherever I go.

It is not often a discussion on spiritual values and truths spontaneously breaks out. I find letters of mine to the newspapers do not have as ready an acceptance when strong on the spiritual. At times, even a lesser spiritual overtone is muted or deleted and the point I wish to make, that I consider the most important, just doesn't get a chance. Writing that keeps to the usual intellectual channels fares rather better, although at times I manage to break through the usual restraints of editorial intentions, much to my delight and surprise.

So with something as important as spiritual discovery, why the reticence to approach it openly, without awkwardness as if it is something untouchable, not a subject fit for daily discussion like we would any other topic of interest? What could be more fruitful or rewarding to humans than this? It brings human nature out into the open, encourages the exploration of the human expression on every level. Not only intellectual, which is merely the introductory stages; but practically, because it leads to a deeper understanding of the human background, its motives and behaviour, its relationship to society, to the environment, to ideas, morality, to everything in fact that humans are and do. What could be more important?

I am delighted to meet people who are interested and moving this way. They are alive in a very special way. To read books by those who are truly awake is likewise uplifting. Even though self-exploration is a journey of joy and heartbreak, smooth sailing at times and rough going at others, I wouldn't have missed it for the world, regardless of whatever else society has to offer in its place. To live with the blessing of the Universal Strangeness is out of this world. Out of mind too. Nothing can match what it brings into human living. You want peace? It brings it. Joy? That too. Insights and understanding into human behaviour like you've never had before and cannot get out of books? Yours to share. And the kind of love you hear talked about. Divine love, unconditional love. That comes our way too.

Where in the arrangements of mankind, of the mind and its organisations, can you be sure of anything like this? You have to yield the self in the process of realisation. So what? This is the troublemaker of time, the cause of our problems and dilemmas in life. Wherever the self raises its obstinate head, there you will find all the problems of life, the difficulties, the injustices, the wars, everything that disrupts harmony and the expression of gentle, caring qualities. So why not part with it and let the Sunshine of Life in? What have you got to lose? Only the troublesome side of human nature.

What do you gain? The warmth, the love, the sweetness of life, the song of the Sunshine breaking out. Simplicity and directness take over from complications and deviousness. It is the end of the rocky road with its bumps and bruises and on to the open highway of life without hang-ups and pileups. Living with the Sunshine is flying with the birds, not crawling underground like worms. That's great for worms but not for humans.

We were meant for the best life has to offer. It comes gift-wrapped in love, bound in understanding, aglow with wisdom and it's yours if you deeply want it. Don't hesitate. Reach out with all you've got, with all you are. Give to this your mind, your heart, your time, interest and attention. Don't hold back. This is the Great Unknown. Leave the safety and security of time. Step off with no haven in sight. Let the heart lead. Don't be timid. Love is waiting, the Sunshine is waiting. Join the happy people who have already made it there. Come back singing, resplendent in the lustre of the Sunshine. This is not a pipedream. This is for real. Go and find out for yourself. There is no other way. You are the Sunshine and the way. May your endeavours be blessed.

❧❧

RIGHT UNDERSTANDING

UNDERSTANDING FLOWS EFFORTLESSLY out of enlightened beings. It is not intellectual but it uses this as a means of conveyance. Truth is always truth — always consistent. The means of expression change but not truth.

As the early means of mechanical conveyance and flight were one thing in the early stages, only to be superseded by later models, so the means of intellectual conveyance change to keep in tune with changing concepts of language. The nature of what is being conveyed is eternal. It is not of the mind, not of concepts.

Encouragement is given through thought, through written and spoken expression. The intention? To awaken desire and give a focus to those who aspire. The seeker creates the approach. Understanding guides the approach. As understanding develops and deepens, so the approach changes. When understanding is what it should be the approach ends. It is not needed any more.

The journey undertaken is created by thought, continues while given impetus by thought, and ends when thought ends. It is a journey through the maze created by thought in its desire to come to a culminating point.

Thought projects a mental Mount Everest to give its movement a greater emphasis. The mountain withdraws only when thinking withdraws. Thought and what it sets out to do go hand in hand. There is not one without the other. Lodged in explanations, ways and means, thought stays there, exercises itself at will, admires its own movement and reassures itself as to the importance of effort and endeavour.

Right understanding deals with all of this, cleans out the confusion thought creates. Thought then abides in right understanding, becomes its willing servant, a pliant extension of that understanding. Right understanding is natural, spontaneous. It flows from moment to moment. There is no explanation for it. It is. When thought abdicates its role as master, right understanding naturally arises.

It's like the rising of the sun. When the world of thought turns and sinks out of sight, the sun of right understanding shines through and lights up the way to clearer, saner, enlightened living.

✌✍

WHY ASK?

WHAT USE IS it to ask the why and wherefore? Birds fly, grasses grow without fuss or bother. Only man torments himself with questions.

Life goes on regardless. Does life, the universe need reasons for its existence? Or is this the invention of the human mind, bent on understanding in this way?

Apart from man, life does not reason why. There is birth, growth, decay and death. But the system goes on and on. Only man suffers the torment of an inquisitive reason.

So everything is wrapped in reason and man is satisfied. Sometimes I wonder if modern man belongs to the natural order of things — or is he an aberration?

Long ago, before his present state of displacement he was close to the earth and the sky, to the seasons, to the green world and the sea. Then he broke away and became civilised with all its attendant problems and deep sense of separation.

Now technologically competent and reason wise he seems lost in an alien world, divorced from the wonder that surrounds him. More's the pity. His mind is ever busy and overflowing with movement.

But what of the heart, of that inner need to return to the magic that once he knew? When the Springtime of Life was ablaze with wonder and he walked in kinship with all that surrounded him and asked no questions of why and what.

For there was no need for this. He was at one with the All That Is and that was all that mattered. All else was secondary and of lesser consequence to the expanded state of his exalted being.

ৡড়

MAKE WAY FOR LIFE

ARTH IS HOME to all its living forms. The mountain ranges, the rivers, the oceans and continents are all part of that home. Air and sunlight are also a vital part. Nature provides what is needed for all its living forms. To human eyes the wonder of it is very complex and amazingly variable.

Wherever they are, plant and animal life have carved out a niche, a corner where they flourish. For plant life many are the means by which they continue and spread. Seeds are carried by birds, spores by the wind, burrs in animal fur. So life goes on.

The blending of life with its environment is a matter of agreement among humans. Could it be otherwise? This is what they appear in, whatever the medium — earth, water, air. All draw from the surroundings. They take what is there, they give back what they are. It all works beautifully unless interfered with by man, who is also part of the show but capable of great disruption.

There are barriers that contain the living forms so development and blending are obviously different from one part to another. Vast mountain ranges and the oceans form great barriers. Deserts too.

Life that takes to the air has great mobility. Which brings us to the habitat. This does not seem to be a barrier in the ordinary sense, yet where plant and animal life has settled into a particular environment, it blends in, thrives there and fades out when the environment is radically altered.

The habitat is important to the presence of life on this planet. In fact, it forms part of the composite picture of what we take life to be. Left to itself, without interference from man, there is still change. Forms have been discarded, new ones take over. That is nature's purpose.

Through all its forms nature is resilient. It has no favourites apart from man who has been blessed with a higher capacity. With the growing impact and spread of mankind the ecology of the planet has been disrupted to a marked degree.

Plant and animal life, even the earth, slept blissfully undisturbed for ages. Enter man the mover, the digger into the earth, who clears large tracts of bushland for home;, the traveller who spans continents, who transports animals and plants across oceans and establishes them in environments where otherwise they couldn't go. So we have invasive plants and animals.

Nature accepts all, regardless of what follows. If creatures or plants become extinct through man's movement — so be it. Mankind looks on and sees the results of its handiwork. Many are stirred from the heart to preserve what nature has fashioned for a particular area. Perhaps they feel intuitively that nature has more wisdom than man — that what she has created is worth preserving, that her creatures and plants are too precious to destroy willy nilly according to man's whim.

There is something about natural habitats, about plants and animals indigenous to an area that is just right — that has appeal, is as it ought to be. There is a side in mankind that is sensitive, that recognises this.

There is also a ruthless side, an arrogant side, a side that brooks little opposition to its determinations whatever these should be. This side has been in control for thousands of years. It rides roughshod over the earth, over its fellow man, over nature's creations.

In moving to restore long years of damage, to restore what we can of the environment, to preserve what we can of fading species (animals, plants and even indigenous cultures), this side must be dealt with or there will always be formidable opposition to the directives of the heart.

It is from this side that damage and disruption emerge to spread over the earth. In man it begins — in man it must end. When disorder reigns in man, so it spreads out to cover the earth. When order takes over, so this too spreads outwards.

The key to environmental protection lies inwards. Outer study there must be. Legislation too is necessary and education of a kind like never before. Government, industry and people need to come together and acknowledge the urgency. A great awakening is needed. It will take more than science, more than politics, more even than a willingness to act.

Surface action is guided from within. It is here, in the inner reaches of our being that the initiative must come from a spiritually transformed mankind. In this we are blended together as one unit concerned with the welfare of mankind, the earth and all its plants and creatures.

We will move as one, each in one's own way, doing what the inner bids. And because the ruthless side has been tamed by the inner light, so it will not interfere and the actions that follow will be right actions. No more can we do then, than what follows.

❧

RESTORING BALANCE

I T'S GO, GO, go in the world of space and time. Action is the name of the game. And when people tire of the energy outpouring then it's time to sleep, to rest, to meditate or to do whatever appeals in the way of stillness. A gentle unhurried walk by the ocean amid natural surrounds, listening to restful music or sitting in a sheltered corner of the garden reading a book or just looking at the trees and plants, at birds — these are the ways in which people withdraw a little from the busy world of the mind.

There is a deep need for balance. Nature has its rhythm and we are a part of this. Deep rest restores the imbalance caused by an excess of action, of too much thinking and doing, of constantly dealing with concerns and demands. When body and feelings incline towards rest, 'tis best to listen and put aside the restless agitation of the mind.

But the mind finds it hard to let go. There is this to be done, that to be attended to — so much is important to the mind. What an appetite for doing when the self is abroad in time. The wellbeing of the body is disregarded, inner needs are ignored and things start to go wrong. Impatience creeps in, sickness gains a toehold and spreads, resistance grows as inwardly there is a pulling away from all the pushing and reaching out, from the wear and tear that follows.

So many find it difficult to stop and restore the balance. Moving in harmony, with thoughts, feelings and body blending into an unhurried, untroubled expression that reflects the natural rhythm of a life in tune with the universal is a life lived to the full. In this there is no breaking away by the mind and feelings, by erratic desires to take over, by the self to overreact through its various functions.

A togetherness prevails to ease aside the diverse movements that spread out on the surface and dissipate energy in so many directions. What the self scatters, the inner unifies. It heals the excesses of the mind, assuages the ravages of bruising feelings and smooths out the tensions that develop. This it does because it is the Great

Healer, capable of instantly diagnosing what ails its human children and supplying the antidote to mental and emotional disarrangement. It does this by sharing what it is, by drawing the estranged self into the Universal Fold for a brief moment that has magical and mystical power.

Little use trying to explain the unexplainable. When it happens, the Sunshine of Life breaks through to irradiate the barren desert that is the self. The walls of our self-made prisons are shattered and that which was serving a life sentence in time is released from its bondage. Understanding saturates the self with a new light. The darkness of ignorance retreats. The self comes alive with expanded awareness, not restricted now to an isolated standpoint but sharing a Universal Oneness that encompasses all.

ॐ

ELUSIVE SILENCE

W HAT BUSY MOVERS we are. So much going on through all the avenues open to us. In sport, so much thinking, planning and effort to win, win, win. So much excitement from supporters, or disappointment if a team loses. All angles studied to maintain a high level of fitness, to overcome injuries. All stations go in the chosen directions.

In politics, it's constant rhetoric, self-congratulations and savage criticism of the opposition — or vice versa. In the work-a-day world, production lines hum with activity. Shop windows fill with fresh produce for the selling: tasty breads, rolls, cakes, steaming cups of coffee, tea, fruit and vegetables, whatever you prefer. Eager people line up to select what they want.

Movement back and forth in the supermarkets: mums pushing strollers with a little one strapped in, other children in tow; shopping trolleys packed high or low with groceries, children running around having fun, maybe one crying wanting its own way. Harried mother scolding, urging the child to be quiet. Motor traffic flowing along the roads, trucks carrying essentials, buses conveying passengers, so many cars in motion. Traffic lights turn red, then green or amber in between. Traffic stops, starts or hurries through.

So it goes, mind and body in movement filling in the time, doing what desire decrees, urging on to planned objectives, or just purposeless rambling with no particular end in view except the doing of something, anyway. So much motion, thinking, energy outflowing, so much feeling released. A restless search to take care of the self, its needs and more — an urgency to lift out of the doldrums of everyday living into the excitement, the enjoyment of entertainment, for contentment or satisfaction. Perhaps the aim is to be a top achiever. Then, if one is exhausted by the outflow, a place to rest, to potter in the garden, listen to favourite music, go into natural surrounds and soak in the quietness, or down to the ocean to walk in the sunshine and feel fresh breezes ease out the stresses and strains of daily living.

The human race is a driven race — driven for more and more. There is always something else to be done, a new avenue to be explored. With the Earth conquered, it was on to the moon, then the planets, after that the stars. In sport, one championship flag or a top trophy gained, then it's all eyes on the next, then the next, ad infinitum. There is no end to the demands of the mind. A millionaire makes the first million, then on to the second and so on. Grow, expand, achieve.

Do we ever pause to question what drives us so? Do we ever tire of the constant drive, the ebb and flow, the highs and lows of success and disappointments? How much longer are humans going to go on like this? As the older ones tire and retire from work, sport or whatever, so the young step in to carry the flag of energetic achievers. The overall movement goes on; humanity on the march, moving to the desires, the demands of the mind, along the avenues that stretch from the past into the present then on to the future.

In all this, there have been rearrangements, readjustments but no deep shift of understanding from a surface level; from living for the sake of the surface self and its extensions to one of reconnecting with the universal level of existence. Stubborn indeed is the intention of the mind to remain locked into the outer, to travel the highways and byways of timeful experience.

The human expression is urging timewards with all the energy it can muster, directing thinking and feeling likewise in this direction. All must serve the god of the self, not the Universal Directive that silently awaits the return of mankind into its eternal fold.

Marching along with physical movement is the perpetual drive of the intellect with its incessant thinking. Always probing, dissecting, analysing, immersed in words and word meaning. This is the main channel the mind travels along. Reason fore and aft, reason all around, reason pouring out like an avalanche on the move — outwardly as chatter-talk, inwardly as thinking but much the same thing, one public, the other private.

Reason storms across the planet, interwoven with every human endeavour. The mind lives, breathes and has its being in reasonable thought. Right thoughts, wrong thoughts, it doesn't matter so long as they are thoughts. The mind feels alive through thinking, through reasonable expression. Where is there mind without reason, without chatter-talk? Where reason is absent, or random thoughts, there, there is silence, or close to it. Absent every movement from the mind and the silence deepens. Allow this to be and the mind fades out of the picture and the silence takes over.

What kind of silence? Do not ask. Put the question, seek an answer and reason returns. The silence retreats. Leave the intellect out of it. Give it half a chance and it will storm its way back in. Have you ever known true silence and intellectual barnstorming at one and the same time?

And don't try the trick of muzzling the intellect through effort just to discover the meaning of the silence. It doesn't work. It is artificial, contrived, not genuine. It's like muzzling a chatterbox to stop chatter-talking. Underneath, the words are bursting to come out. Silence is only golden when it's natural, effortless, when everything leads into it without persuasion or coercion.

Why so much emphasis on the silence? Because in silence we learn the truth about human nature, about what it is. Any meaning given to the silence will be wrong unless you become one with the silence, dwell in it completely for a moment. That's when you learn the true meaning of the silence. Not in thinking about it, imagining it or trying to bring it about through mental posturing. That's like making a house out of plasticine to live in: it's worthless.

Listen with your mind to the words if you will, graft your own meaning and the silence will pass you by. Rather, listen with your whole being, come together in a oneness. No distinction or levels in you, no sense of separation, of being here, there or anywhere. No endeavour by the mind in any way. Drop being an observer. Then the silence 'is'. No location, no time involved, no whisper from the mind to cause distractions. If you are puzzled, so be it. If you want to go back to the drawing board of effort, remain in techniques or whatever else appeals, do so, but do not expect to shift out of the ordinary into the super state of the silence.

The silence embraces all — in silence. Be silent then.

ೲ

IS IT SO?

W E HEAR THAT all is one — all is consciousness. We look at our surroundings, at the trees, earth, sky and to the surface sight this does not seem possible.

Looking back, we erupted on the scene, an infant body expelled from the womb at the time of birth. We do not know where we are or where we come from. For months we listen and look our way to learning, to settling into the body, family and our surroundings.

We grow, learn language and thinking, draw on the collective experience of mankind. Early on there is a playtime in our lives and little we care about the why or wherefore of life — only that we are here. We want to enjoy life so we shy away from pain and trouble as best we can.

Somehow, it seems to pursue us wherever we go, whatever we do. Still, we manage to enjoy the fun time, the young time as long as we are loved and looked after and disruptions do not come our way.

Physical maturity comes. So does question time if we are inclined toward discontent and to be a searcher of life's elusive mysteries. Having settled into intellectual analysis with its 'why this?' and 'why that?' and absorbing the collective explanations of philosophy, religion and science, we become rather knowledgeable — full of words, ideas and meanings.

The deeper we try to penetrate into life's mysteries the more we lose ourselves in complex explanations. Driven by an insatiable desire to shift from the dream self to the absolute, we move on, trying visualisation, meditation, mental exercises to break through the fog of ignorance that surrounds the mind.

Search for the light — discover truth — awaken out of the timeful dream — be at one with the Universal. We wriggle and twist like a fish on a hook, longing to be free, to live without concerns and doubts. We want to be free flowing in our self-expression without the hindrances of fear and uncertainty.

But it seems while the mind is abroad as the self, the seeker, the body, reaching out for whatever, for this, that or anything else it aims for, then disappointment is imminent. There is no lasting satisfaction for the self in timeful establishment. Outer palaces, inner palaces built by the mind, are temporary abodes. They are ephemeral like mirages cast on the sand. A shift in perception, a change and the apparent security vanishes. Self-created, they have no lasting reality.

The mind works like a beaver seeking the unknown. Eager to join the Timeless One, it dedicates itself to the search — bathes itself in the atmosphere of meditation, reading, ashrams, whatever it considers is conducive to its search. While it is abroad as a centre of distinction it is still in the field of the self, the little one who is trapped in distinction, living the illusion of separation.

Mighty are the struggles of the self to be free of ignorance, of the timeful trap. It remains entrapped. There is no intellectual ladder to freedom. Wherever the self is, there is self-delusion. Only when the self is not, is there freedom and the end of illusion, ignorance and separation.

The self was born to know distinction, to limit itself to body, name and what have you — to juxtapose itself to its surroundings. Yet it will move heaven and earth to make its way to the absolute.

The wise self listens. It doesn't jump to conclusions, takes nothing for granted, asks for nothing, expects nothing. It does not limit itself through action and ideas. It's not going anywhere nor does it expect a treasure trove of returns at the end of the rainbow of investigation.

It's travelled all the highways and byways of effort projected by the mind. Searched them through from beginning to end and found nothing of value there.

So it dropped into a stillness. In this, effort vanished — self and surroundings disappeared. In that silence, something extraordinary happened. The Absolute had taken over.

∽✑✑∼

BEYOND SELF

WHERE HAS SIMPLE enjoyment gone now-a-days? Just think about it. Notice how many have drifted apart into a deeper isolation due to differing lifestyles and accelerating intellectual development yielding so much more in the way of material possessions and technological gadgets. There is so much variety to make life interesting, and financial arrangements for protection when things go wrong, such as health benefits and social services.

Yet still, where is the joy in day to day living, in the little things we do, the ordinary experiences that follow, one after the other? Not the big, exciting things some set out to do — a trip around the world, climb a mountain, a night out to a special function, attend an important event — but the little things that go on day after day.

Life is full of such little things — listening to a rooster crow in the distance, greeting the day in the way it knows best; splashing the face in cold water on a nippy winter's morning; walking out into a new day, whether to go shopping or to work. You know, all the ordinary things we do to fill in the day.

Why does living seem so dull if we do not have something special to give us a lift? Notice the deep, cool, satisfied way smokers inhale on cigarettes; the eager rush to go somewhere we've been looking forward to for some time, to a special event, the weekend, or holidays? We look forward to coming events to brighten our living, to lift jaded spirits, to involve and absorb the mind's attention. Anything to get away from dullness, from the disinterest that develops toward ordinary, everyday living.

Talk about grasshoppers on the move. We are jumping away from facing ourselves as fast as we can. Urging toward future events to get away from a boring present. Always around the corner lies the solution to our emptiness, our problems and difficulties. There are better times ahead, perhaps some new discovery, another relationship, or arrangements that will make us happier and take care of the complex difficulties that disturb us today.

Struggles to the right, to the left, all around. The mind reaching out in every direction — for what? For some means to deal with troubled lives and regain joy without disruption. We want to breeze through life on a highway of fun, laughter and happy togetherness. And what happens? We bog down in complicated technicalities, in the how to do this, in methods, in the constant meanderings of the mind. Everyone holding to their own little corner of the world, protecting the interests of number one, seeking to advantage themselves, giving little away without expecting some kind of return.

So in the international arena it takes weeks, months, years to decide on necessary changes. I'll disarm if you will, throw away a plane if you do the same, defuse one of my atomic devices if you match me. Consensus? What a laugh, what a complex coming together. You give a little of this and in return we'll yield a little of what we have. With watchfulness at all times and suspicion that one side may gain too much and the other side lose in the process. Such fragile accords when humans come together to heal deep rifts and divergent outlooks.

Breakdowns all the time. High hopes at the beginning, then the rot sets in and goes from one person to another, from organisation to organisation, from nation to nation. The self sets the seeds of protection and security. How the plants flourish, well fed by prejudice and fear, by human wiles and stubborn intellects. Then comes the harvest of disarray, of divisions and discord. How long will humans continue like this — buoyed up by great expectations one moment then bogged down by the reality of unrelentingly separate standpoints? Endless confrontations, constant bickering, savage barrages of criticism. Isn't anyone happy anymore?

Advanced societies sit on a technological barrel bursting at the seams with useful and attractive contents. Enough can be produced for everyone to have a fair share but the demand of the mind for more — more for the 'me', not for you — is spoiling the fun, the harmony that should be ours to enjoy.

There's more in so many directions. More money, security, protection, profits, possessions, entertainments, excitement, sensation. Mind on the move, working, inventing to fill its inner emptiness with what it needs to reassure and support itself. God, how empty we are without these things, without possessions and secure social and national arrangements as a means of protection from fear and insecurity.

Mind, expanding in time, reaching out through organisations, nations, individually through any means for a place in the sun. Not just any place to warm a backside, but a more advantageous one, a superior one. And so, struggle, struggle, struggle — one against one, many against many, nation against nation. Talking peace, cooperation, togetherness and getting nowhere, because the inner tendency for disruption has never been faced and dealt with so it comes to an end in everyone. When it dies in the individual it has no further outlet. It cannot disrupt humans coming together for any worthwhile purpose.

Talk cannot kill it. Intention will not bring it to an end, although it is a beginning. But discovery will. Discovery and the fresh understanding this brings. Discovery of what? Discovery of the Universal Nature the mind shares in like manner with all. In discovery there is integration and whoever shares in this is born anew, is ready to forge new relationships in the outside world. Relationships based on spiritual foundations, not on those created by a divided mind.

When humans learn what they are and what they have in this way, they will not grasp so strongly for outer riches, nor will they struggle one against the other. There is a richness of a different kind within. Monetary worth, possessions, although given their due, cannot compare in value with it. Its coming rekindles the sparkle driven out by dullness and resurrects the joy in living. The Sunshine of Life is abroad, arousing the mind into a fresh appreciation of the living process.

What problems can trouble the self when it finally wakes to its true potential, when the inner capacity is on the move without hindrance from a self-centred mind bent on self-preservation? Back comes the fun in living. Out go the woes. The timeless magician is with us. Its wand touches everything into sparkling splendour. It brings the spiritually dead back to life, rejuvenates, regenerates, reawakens the mind from its long, dark sleep and makes us whole again.

No more will we wander the highways of time like lost sheep looking for sustenance and protection, suspicious that there is a ravenous wolf behind every bush waiting to devour us. The directive we need is within, not outside, not in reason, nor in the mind's arrangements, pleasant and comfortable though these may be, but deep within. Beyond the isolation of the self, beyond the flow of reason, beyond the mind's separate and avid grasp.

Go there, meet it, learn for yourselves; and in learning, life yields its greatest significance, fulfils its highest purpose. You will gain all you need to make of living a happy, carefree togetherness with a minimum of disruption from any direction.

❧❦

IN THE HEARTBEAT OF
NATURE

I N LIVING THE human experience, people often have to face difficulties of various kinds. Whatever the nature of the upsets, those affected work their way through as best they can, with or without help. Disturbances may come to anyone — to the rich and seemingly invulnerable and those who have little. To a thoughtful observer it may seem there is little justice in the way some are called on to experience unbearable pain and a shattering run of difficulties.

Sicknesses, sometimes needing a series of operations or courses of medical treatment that leave sickening side effects; relationships that leave one partner carrying a heavy burden while the other turns into a wastrel, a drunkard, a wife beater or is often elsewhere contributing little to the relationship. Sometimes, harsh treatment is handed out by the forces of nature, by storm, earthquake, volcanic eruptions, drought, or fires that burn over vast areas of bushland, razing houses, killing stock and taking human life as well.

People may be on the receiving end of violence from fellow humans. Robberies, murders, rapes — aggressive attacks with little or no provocation. All these, the pain and the violence, the extreme poverty many endure, the battling loner trying to look after a family and make a dollar stretch into two, makes the thoughtful wonder what is going on in this world.

This list of extreme hardship, of excessive brutality could be extended endlessly. So many with very little, yet others with more than they need. Expensive and elaborate homes, an overload of personal possessions, jewellery, artworks worth a fortune, people living in the lap of luxury; while others eke out a precarious existence, living in tin shacks, under hessian bags or sleeping in the streets, in parks, anywhere they can. The poor are often weak with hunger, racked by coughs, tormented with sickness. With spirits low, they wait till death calls and brings an end to their misery. Or until compassionate humans with health intact and the inclination to do something move in to lend a hand and help the unfortunate ones out of the furrows of misery the plough of life has prepared for them, sometimes for a weary lifetime of hardship and pain.

It is the seeming inequality of what humans have thrust upon them, or perhaps bring upon themselves, that is so disturbing to those who reflect seriously on the matter. We may, if we are well off, ignore the difficulties others are enduring and enjoy the lifestyles we have adopted. We may close our eyes to what is happening to others, not only in our own societies but also in other countries out of our immediate sight. We may donate according to our means or generosity to a worthwhile cause. Then when the giving is over, we may lapse back to our accustomed pursuits and give little thought to the situations others are caught up in; to why these continue and why it is that humans, who are so capable of extensive organisation, of technical and agricultural productivity, are yet so unable to rapidly change the status quo for the better even though the knowledge and the skill to do so is readily available.

The intention is there by concerned individuals, by government and international organisations formed to respond to emergencies and disasters. But thus far humans have not been able to translate ideas, money, equipment and skills into effective action that gradually overcomes the tragic situations so they do not recur. International and charitable organisations keep working away, improving a little here and there. Yet still a deluge of tragedies continues, threatening to engulf mankind in misery, leaving many despairing the tide of poverty, violence and death will never come to an end.

Must mankind go on, day after day, year after year, crippled in its approach to the problems it faces? The experts say the means are at hand — the knowledge, the equipment, the skilled personnel and the money (so much wasted on armaments and maintaining vast armies). We have or can manufacture everything that is needed but we cannot put this into operation immediately and effectively. What is the holdup?

Look at the time, money, technical skill, production and organisation poured into the armed forces. This we do, year after year, willingly or unwillingly, upgrading weapons regardless of cost. Vast sums of money are poured into gambling, into amusements that yield little of worthwhile value, or useless habits that impair health. But we cannot supply what is needed to educate those who lack the knowledge to alleviate their distressing situations and become self-sufficient in what they must have if they are to enjoy life. Everything is available except the will to give and share and so humans move along the highway of life, some smoothly, others slowly, many crawling or limping along and with millions at a standstill with little motion at all.

When are the winds of change going to blow through the human populations on this earth? Not only the economic winds, the technological winds, the winds of innovation and knowledge, the winds of changing ideas and moral redirection, but the wind of spiritual togetherness, of sharing and caring. The wind that will lift mankind out of its self-centred apathy and indulgence and move them together as one people, each giving what they have and what they are, in common purpose: the preservation and enhancement of the human experience, making of it a gentle and sensitive expression of harmony, sharing and learning.

On the surface, there is the means to do what must be done. Inwardly, there is the capacity to release the energy and the understanding to get things moving in the right direction. The mind sees what needs to be done, even has the knowhow. But mankind apparently cannot release the inner capacity to generate movement, maintain momentum and balance so humans do not lose their way and degenerate into squabbling sections, with each grinding against the other, economically, ideologically, politically, religiously or in any other divisive way the mind can devise.

The mind, no matter how earnest its endeavours or sincere its intentions, cannot peacefully change the world or people without the ongoing participation of the inner spiritual capacity. Unless they have had clear evidence of the existence of the spiritual and experienced the effects of its advent on the psyche they will not be aware of what it can do. This is a no-go area, a non-existent nature to those who have not shared the spiritual and the awakening it brings. This capacity is common in all humans, rich or poor, educated or not.

Over thousands of years, many have lived without spiritual contact, so human progress has been and still is unbalanced. Because of the lack of spiritual awareness, humanity breeds fear, aggression, acquisitiveness and moves in strange and unhealthy directions. Technologically, the mind is bolting ahead, expanding and becoming more expert and experienced, but inwardly a most important aspect of human nature is remaining rather static and underdeveloped.

Humans lack true direction in living. They work to serve the ideas and arrangements of the mind, bodily needs and to satisfy the emotions in pleasurable ways. Blinded by material progress, growing expertise and increasing knowledge, the values they live by lack spiritual substance and there is little, if any, awareness of this. Lift your sights away from immediate self-involvement, observe without bias what is going on and you must see the lack of a vital spirit of true togetherness. The aggressive behaviour that does not lessen, the savage assault on flesh, mind and emotions with whatever weapons or words people can lay hand or tongue to.

Those committed to violence hammer away as if life is of little consequence. Women, children, elderly people, anyone who gets in the way. Label them differently, acknowledge them as enemies to make it easier. A blind rampage of evil and sinister intent is on the move. Murderous, mindless, indifferent and callous. A sensitive living experience wasted in the wanton pursuit of psychological and physical security. Little search for the enduring in life, for lasting values, for a deeper meaning. Just give a free rein to the mind to have what it will, do what it will, build as it likes and in the process, don't worry about the damage to the inner. The mind with its ideas is in control, on the move to anywhere it fancies.

Unless self-destruction brings it to a sudden halt. Or the inner spiritual capacity awakens and proceeds to effect a change that will astonish and delight those it touches. They will marvel at the sensitivity that arises, the release of freshness and energy that invigorates living, the interest that renews itself, the sparkle that splashes over everything like sunshine irradiating. The darkness of the mind's behaviour dissolved — its ignorance dissipated. People emerge into the springtime of existence, glowing with an inner radiance. We are Children of the Sunshine, not born of a chance happening but born of a Divine Love. With the spiritual active we are no longer in the service of intentions that have degraded and well nigh destroyed us.

When the spiritual is the sole directive of mankind, no more will evil cast its dark shadow over this troubled planet. It will not have the outlets. Humans will renew their tryst with universal life like secret lovers, meeting it every time as if for the first time. Often they will gaze with wide-eyed wonder at all that is going on around them. They will call to one another with deeper feelings and clearer voices, look without intellectual intervention at the starry skies at night, at the full moon softly shining.

They shall see the Strangeness in everything that is. The hardness and harshness projected by intellectual activity will not raise its head to affect the new sensitivity, nor distort the vision and appreciation that arises. We will have the world our children need to grow up and flourish in and adults too will have all they need to make of life a remarkable adventure in living.

We will finish with these attempts to build enduring foundations in time, with looking for a home in the garden of timeful experience. With the sparkle we'll stay and when the sun shines, we'll shine with it; when the wind blows and the seasons come and go, with these too we shall be. We are in the sounds of birds calling to one another in the springtime, in the hovering of the hawk, in the swoop of the falcon, in the growing grasses. In all these things, we are. Even in the very earth, the mountains and the rivers, the deserts and the forests, the lands of ice and snow.

In the heartbeat of nature we will be established, moving with its rhythm, flowing with its timeless nature, mysteriously absorbed in a seeming non-existence — yet still sharing Being without end.

به‌به

THE HEART IS BEGINNING TO STIR

YEARS AGO, UNSPOILT Bush and clean beaches were not the environmental issues they are today. We had plenty of these to enjoy at will. What we didn't have was prosperity, affluent lifestyles, home ownership or plenty of job opportunities. We were poor in material possessions and money and so, when industrial development began to take off here in the West, we welcomed it with open arms.

We expected and did indeed gain many benefits. We marvelled at the rapid development in many directions — the advent of the modern motor car, the arrival of TV, even gazed in wonder at the night sky as we watched the moving pinpoint of light that heralded the advance into space of the first sputnik.

Then apprehensively we began to realise there was a price to pay. Rapid progress brought pollution, the invasion of our beaches by new industries, the clearing away of natural vegetation and also cars, trucks, motor traffic on the move, noisy, even dangerous at times, and an irresistible demand for more and more roads.

People change over the years, so today we are taking stock and assessing where we are going. We still see the need for economic development but not at the same breakneck pace. Deep down, the urge is growing to ease it off, to preserve what is left of our beaches and bushland and to have more of parks and recreational grounds close to residential areas.

It is not only a growing distaste of pollution or a dislike of traffic and industrial noise that is urging us in this new direction but also a longing for peaceful, green havens where nature reigns supreme and unspoilt. Somewhere we can relax a while away from the hustle, bustle and stresses of everyday living.

This is an insistent demand that is growing year by year. It should not be ignored by town planners for it will grow stronger in the years ahead and will eventually have its way as one of the prime considerations in planning.

Unfortunately, there are still people addicted to industrial expansion regardless, who only see merit in big construction and industrial development, who must send their bulldozers out, hear the chainsaws buzzing or they are not happy.

Sooner or later, a saner balance must prevail. It's time for the human heart to assert its nature, to act as a counterbalance to the demands of the mind for insistent economic expansion. Without the discipline imposed by the heart, the mind runs riot at breakneck speed and the result is constant expansion just for the sake of it and an increasingly affluent lifestyle that multiplies material goods regardless of need or deeper human values.

The sad result is divorce from peaceful surrounds, from restful havens, from the soothing presence of nature as it is in its own delightful way. And this is something that torments the human spirit, harries the mind and grates on the nerves.

Eventually, when humans cannot bear this kind of inner pain any longer, the heart moves to reassert its dominance over the human direction.

Today, in the strong interest that people are showing to preserve the environment and to control the pace and quality of industrial development, we are seeing the beginning of the human heart's resurgence.

လၖက

WE CANNOT GO IT ALONE

WATCHING THE NEWS on TV and reading the newspaper I am reminded of the ills and spills that afflict and affect mankind. There is a host of problems. Violence and aggression continue. There is conflict. The earth is ravaged in the search for riches. Nature strikes back with earthquakes, floods, storms. Fires rage through bushland.

Yet life, ever resilient, goes on. People are battered with pain and loss, with brutal treatment at the hands of violent intruders. The tears flow and despair and bewilderment surface. Then a spark of humanity emerges and others move in to minimise the damage and alleviate the pain.

In spite of widespread turmoil, strife, erratic behaviour and contradictory viewpoints, people rise each morning, tired or fresh, dull or bright, eager or otherwise, to greet another day. The older people take it quietly; the young surge energetically into the social mainstream, eager to experience what life has to offer.

In the meantime, we expect great things from our leaders. They promise much around election time but the mix that is human living goes on, with no end in sight to trouble of some kind.

Put aside what nature brings our way, why is it that humans, with a vast store of knowledge and experience to draw on cannot eradicate the considerable proportion they themselves add to their woes? Why does the human contribution continue as it does?

The human heart longs for rest, peace, joy, for love, for an ever expanding life of delight. Yet the heart is pushed aside by the hard-headed mind, by the desire for power, possessions, riches, by the urge to dominate, to manipulate, to unleash aggression and violence for whatever purpose.

As long as this kind of mind is at the helm of human affairs, the heart isn't given a chance, is not listened to, and love is just a word, something uttered but not allowed expression.

Can humans go it alone, building their social paradises on earth? Or do we need a helping hand from a higher power — a guiding light to show the way?

Religions say 'yes' but somehow the message doesn't get through and mind continues to reign in its own right. Still fondly believing that it can go it alone — that it has the resources of understanding, intellectual acumen, reasonable initiative and intelligence to lead mankind into the sunshine of a better way of life.

But there are some who are convinced otherwise, who have reached out in time of need to touch this higher power, whose longings have been answered and who thereby allow the mind to become subordinate to a new light, to a higher love.

With the insights and understanding that flow in they see why the mind must yield, why the self must be put aside if living is to proceed as it should and harmony set its seeds, grow and flourish to good effect in the human expression.

They learn their lessons the hard way, a step at a time, with every lesson tested and tried in the school of experience and relationships. Not till the ways of the mind are thoroughly understood and the inner channels open wide to the inflow of a higher nature do they rest from their endeavours to wrest from life its most deeply hidden treasure.

And by then, the heart has opened wide to allow affection and love through and the mind has allowed itself to act as servant to a higher directive. One that shows by its light, love and wisdom that it is indeed the only reliable guide for mankind.

༺ঔৈ༻

ABOUT THE AUTHOR

J OSEPH RAFFA WAS born in 1927 in Fremantle, Western Australia. He enjoyed an idyllic childhood roaming the bush and the seashore. In his teens Joseph became a dedicated atheist, looking to science for answers to the riddles of life and the universe. Then, in his early twenties, he experienced a moment of discovery that transformed his life. As Joseph's life opened out spiritually following this awakening, he was inspired to put pen to paper to encourage others to embark on their own journey of discovery.

Joseph died of cancer in 2010, leaving behind a legacy of inspirational writing which is now being made available to a wider audience. Visit www.towardsthesilentheart.com for more information about Joseph and his books.

www.ingramcontent.com/pod-product-compliance
Lightning Source LLC
Chambersburg PA
CBHW070105070426
42448CB00038B/1726